K4 **PRESCHOOL**

EXPLORING GOD'S LOVE

PositiveAction
BIBLE CURRICULUM

Written by Kristi Houser and Mollie Whitley with Champ Thornton

Copyright © 2011, 2014 by Positive Action for Christ, Inc. P.O. Box 700, 502 West Pippen Street, Whitakers, NC 27891.

www.posiitiveaction.org

Second edition 2014
Second printing 2016

Printed in the United States of America

ISBN 978-1-59557-180-9

Edited by C.J. Harris
Design by Shannon Brown
Illustrations: Dana Thompson

Published by

⊘ **PositiveAction**
BIBLE CURRICULUM

Contents

Dear Teacher or Parent,

Thank you for choosing our preschool study, *Exploring God's Love*. Here at Positive Action Bible Curriculum, **it is our prayer that your students will grow in their knowledge of God and their love for Him as they discover the majesty of His glory.** This study will introduce your students to one aspect of that glory–the amazing love of God. They will follow God's loving plan from the creation of the world to its climax in the life, death, and resurrection of Jesus Christ, His Son. If we can be a help to you in this study or future studies, don't hesitate to contact us.

Your friends at Positive Action Bible Curriculum

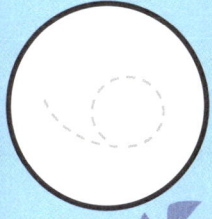

God Made . . .

Trace the number 6. Then paste the animals and Adam and Eve on the land.

God's One Rule

Finish coloring the picture of the Garden. Then cross out the one tree that Adam and Eve were not supposed to eat from.

God's Shining Promise

Color the stars that Abraham saw in the night sky.

Jacob the Trickster

Connect the dots to see Jacob's pot of soup. Color the pot black, the soup red, and the smoke gray.
Then color Jacob and Esau.

God Is with Jacob

Paste the pictures from the story in the order that they happened. Then trace the numbers.

1

2

3

4

5

6

A Change of Heart

Finish coloring the picture.

Showing Kindness

Draw a happy face below the picture if a child is showing kindness. Draw a sad face below the picture if a child is not showing kindness. Then finish coloring the pictures.

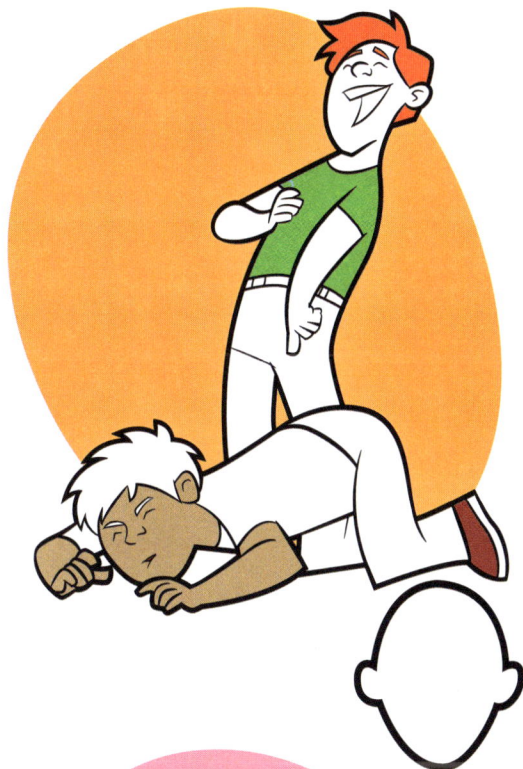

Moses Sees God's Glory

Paste Moses in the cave. Then color the cave.

The Twelve Spies

Fill in the blanks with the correct numbers at the bottom of the page. Then finish coloring the picture.

_____ spies believed God, but _____ did not.

God Takes Care of Me

Color by number.

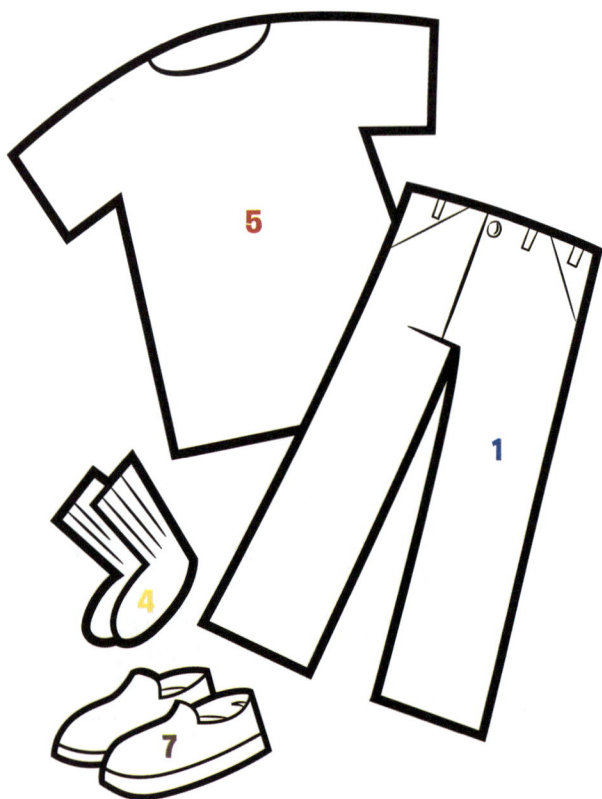

1 = blue

2 = green

3 = purple

4 = yellow

5 = red

6 = orange

7 = brown

Look and Live

Draw a snake on the pole. Then paste in the people who are looking at the snake on the pole.

Following God's Plan

Trace each number. Then color the dotted lines with the same color of each number.

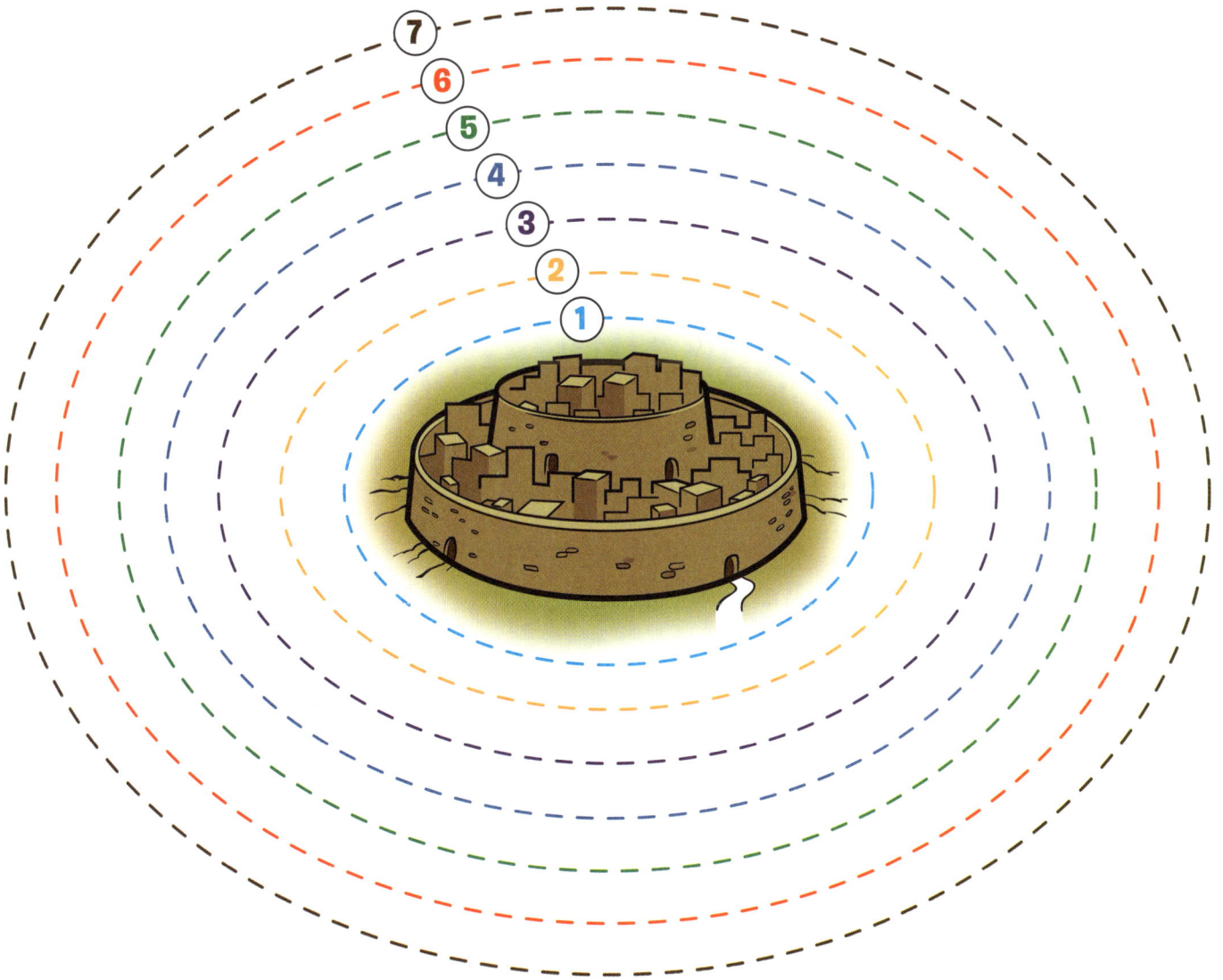

1 2 3 4 5 6 7

For the Lord and for Gideon

Paste the Midianites' tents in the center of the circle. Then color the torches and the horns.

The King's Statue

Connect the dots. Then color Nebuchadnezzar's statue yellow.

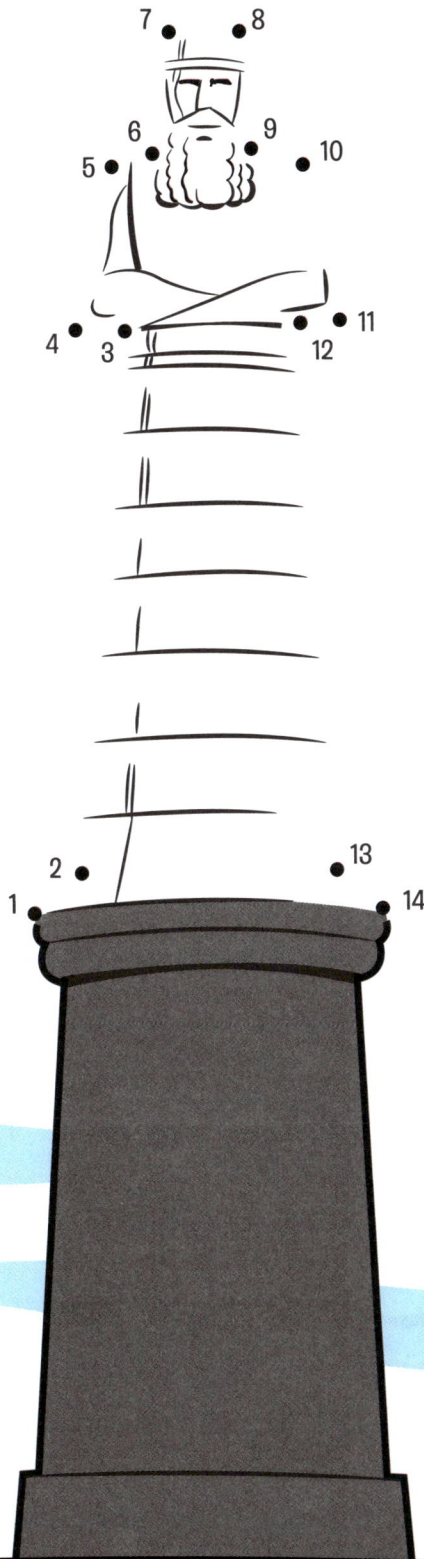

57

Nebuchadnezzar Is Very Angry

Draw King Nebuchadnezzar's tight lips and bulging eyes. Number the flames as you count them to see how much hotter the king was going to make the fire than normal.

58

Going Home

Trace each path to the Promised Land with its matching color.

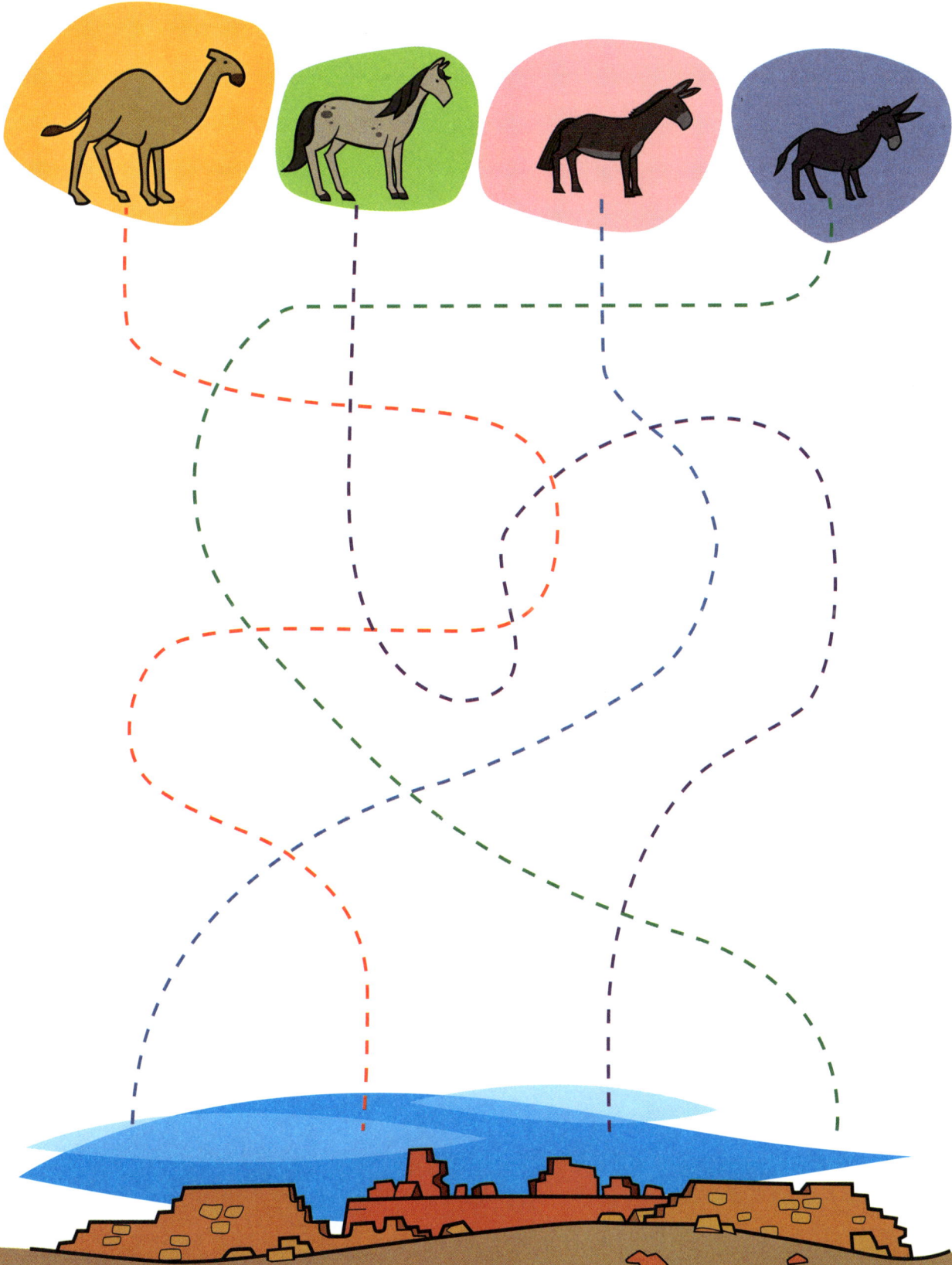

Rebuilding the Temple

Help the Israelites rebuild the Temple by pasting the pieces where they belong on the page

John the Prophet

Draw lines from John to the things that belong to him.

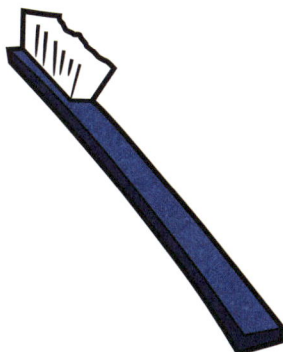

In Line with Sinners

Cut and paste Jesus into the line of people waiting to be baptized.

Doing the Right Thing

Circle the pictures of the children who are making right choices.

Wedding Miracle

Count and number the pots. Then color them.

Putting the Pieces Together

Cut out the puzzle from the cutout page. Then put the pieces together to tell the story of Nicodemus.

Look and Live

Find and color the people who are looking at the pole or at Jesus. Do not color the people who are not looking.

Sharing Jesus' Love

Draw a picture of yourself in the box labeled "Me." Draw a picture of your teacher in the box labeled "My Teacher."
In the small boxes, make a checkmark to show who God uses to share Jesus' love.

Me

My Teacher

Jesus' Healing Power

Trace the letters. Then draw lines to match the "Before" and "After" pictures.

Before

After

Getting to Jesus

Using a crayon, follow the path that the four men took to get their friend to Jesus.

Who Is This Man?

Color by number.

10=grey   11=brown   12=blue   13=green
14=purple   15=yellow   16=red

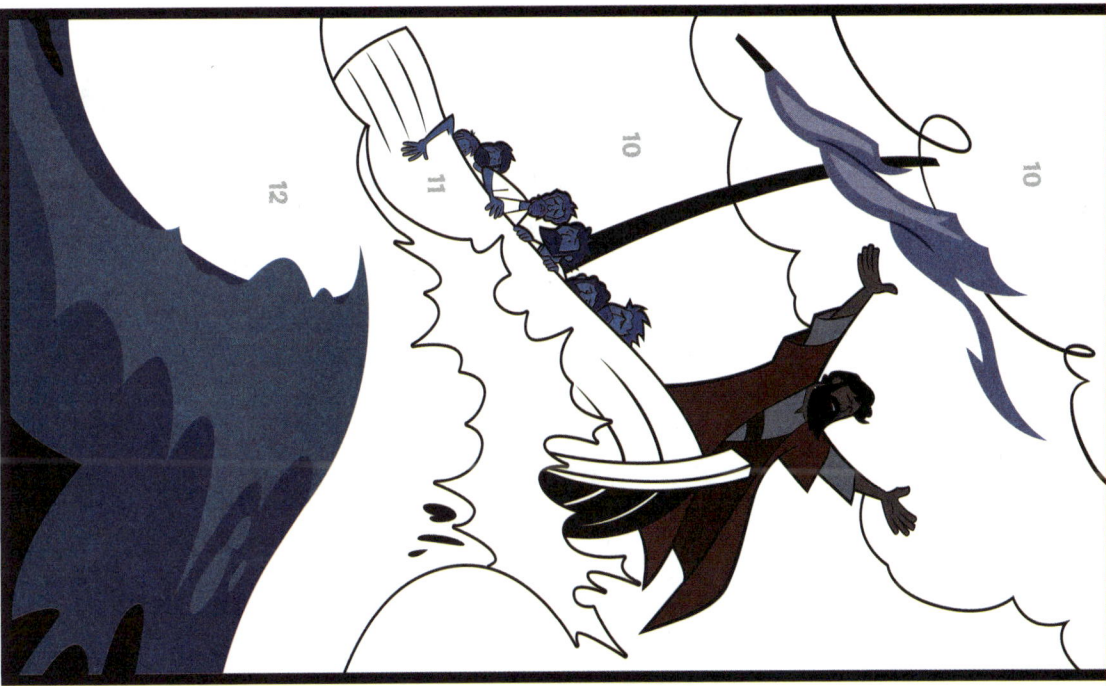

Who Touched Me?

Find and circle the woman touching Jesus' clothes. Then color Jesus' clothes.

Alive Again

Put the scenes of the story in the correct order by writing their numbers in the boxes.

As Good as New

Trace the dots to finish the picture. Then draw the Pharisees' mouths to show how angry they were.

89

I Can See Clearly Now

Finish the picture of what the blind man saw by coloring the sky blue, the building brown, and the robes your favorite color.

Lord, I Believe

Cut out Jesus and the blind man and paste them on the page.

Time to Celebrate

Find and circle Jesus in the crowd of people at Matthew's party. Then color the table and food.

Great Faith

Match the numbers to the pictures to show the correct order of the story.

1

2

3

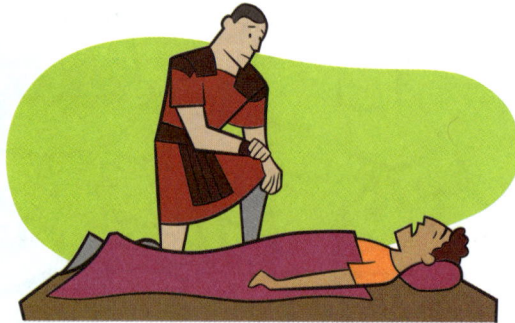

4

Mighty, Powerful, and Glorious

Cut and paste Moses and Elijah beside Jesus. Then draw the beams of light coming from Jesus' face and clothes.

Listen and Obey

On the left side of your paper, draw a picture of your teacher. Draw lines from your teacher to the things you can do to listen and obey.

On Top of the Mountain

Number the pictures in the correct order.

Serving or Selfish?

Circle the pictures of children serving. Cross out the pictures of children being selfish.

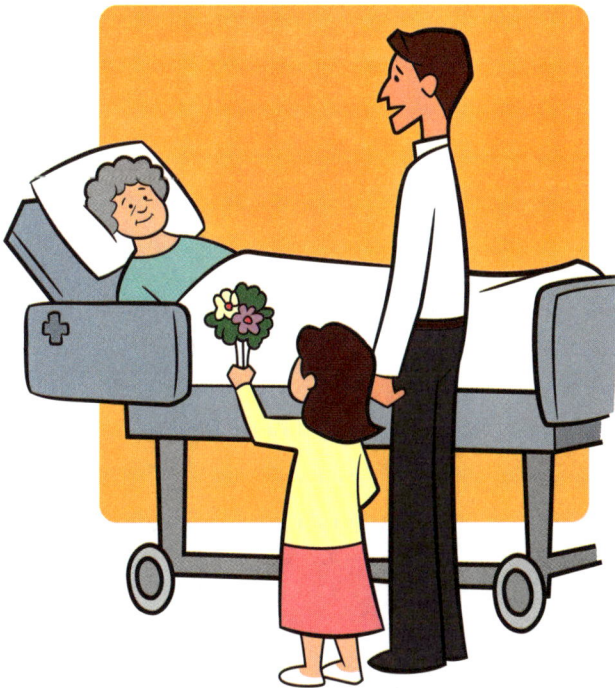

Little Things Count

Count the number of ears of corn and finish the sentence. Then color the picture.

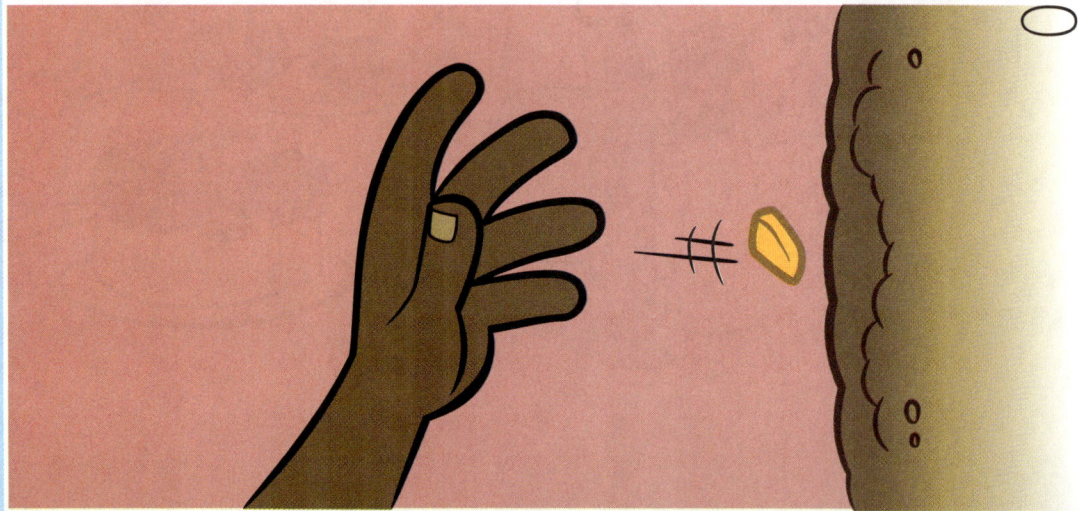

One grain of corn made _____ ears.

Jesus Tells a Story

Draw the rich man and his two sons.

Going Home

Help the son find his way back home to his father.

Welcome Home

Color by letter.

B=brown	**O=Orange**
R=red	**G=green**

God Honors the Humble

Connect the dots. Then finish coloring the picture.

115

The Only Way

Cross out the pictures of the things that will not get you into heaven. Draw a heart around the one picture that shows the only way to heaven.

116

Color the pictures. Then cut on the dotted line and staple the pages in order to make a booklet.

Jesus Heals Lazarus

117

Name: ____________________

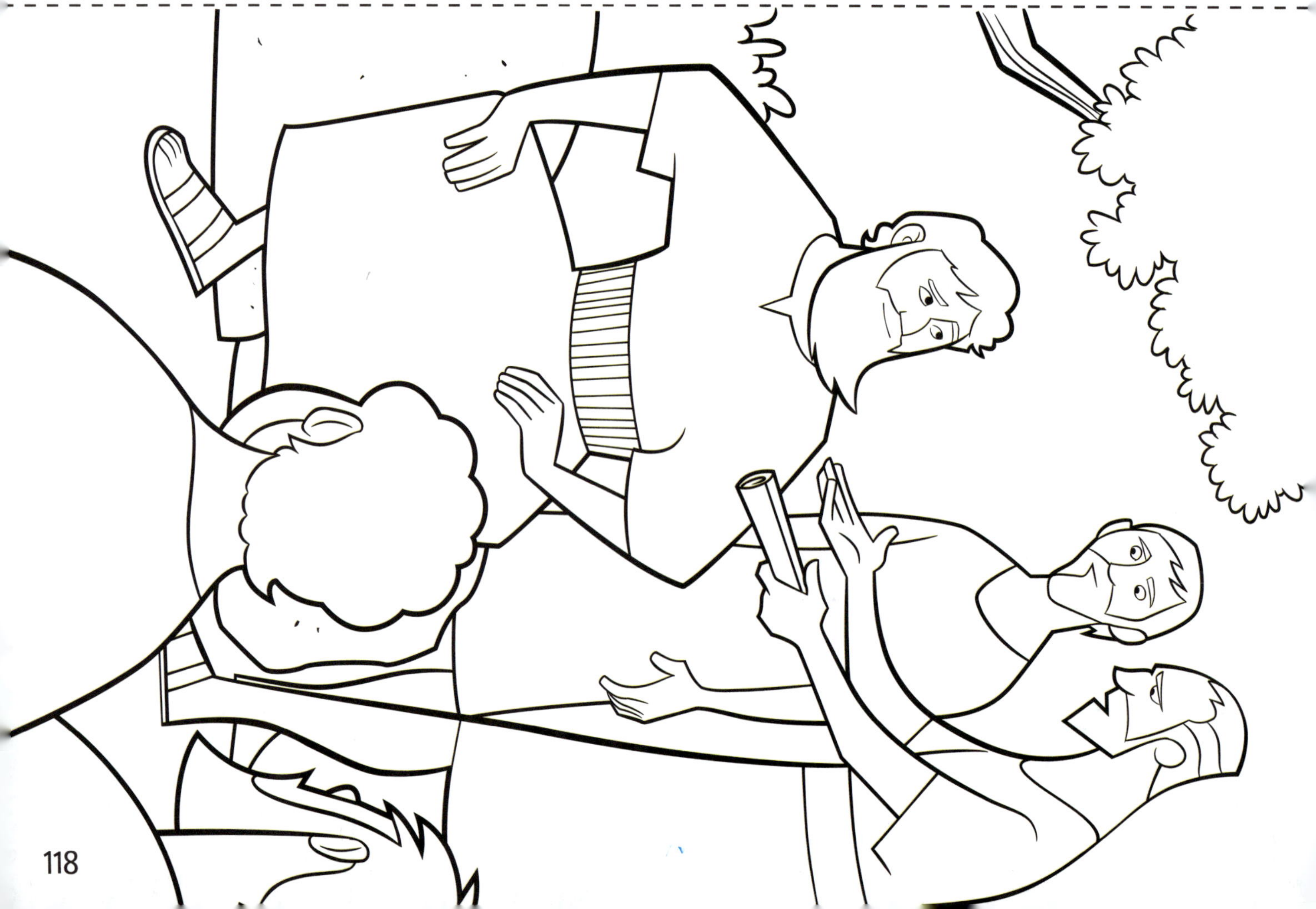

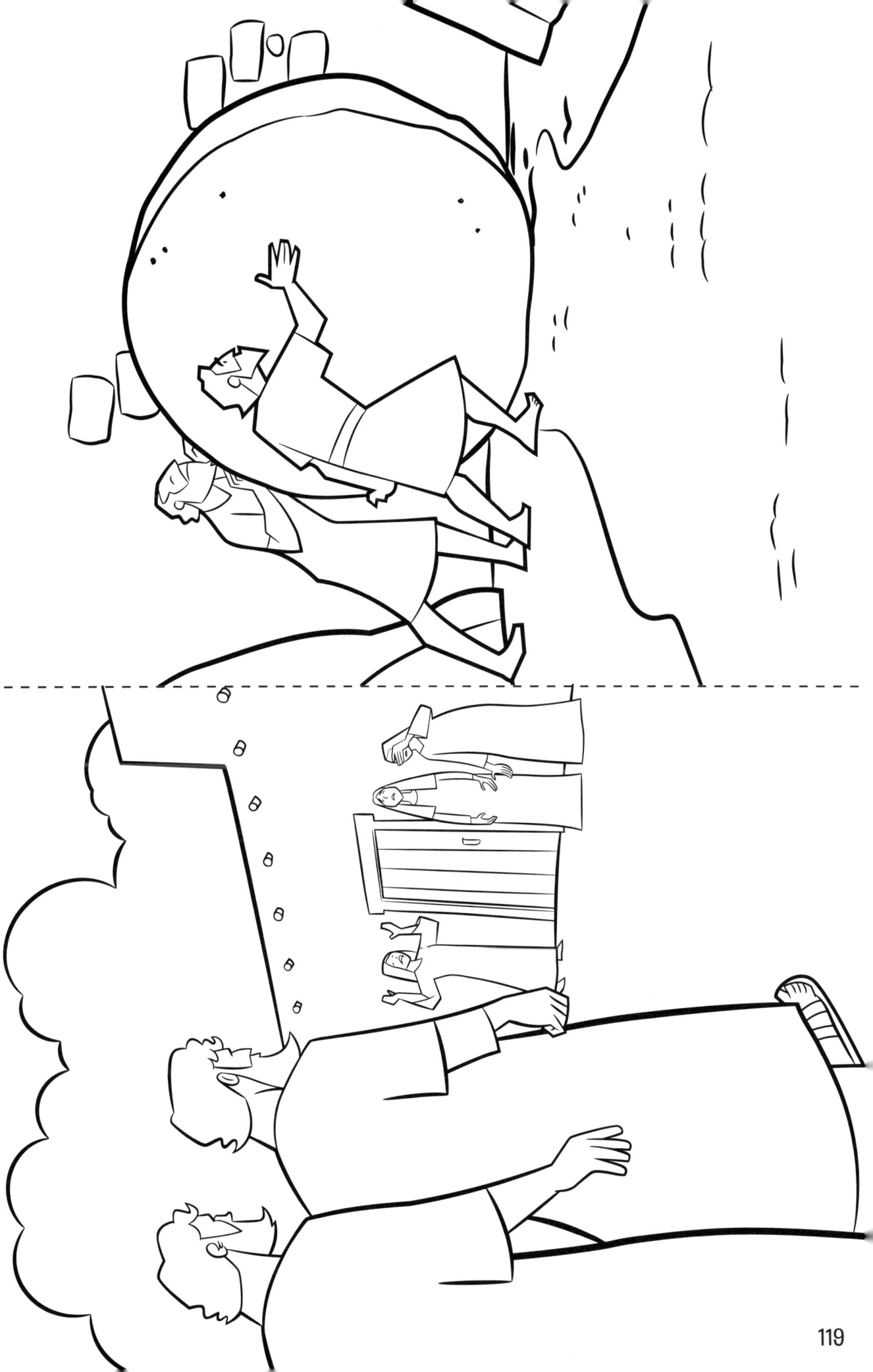

Trying to Trick Jesus

Starting with the letter "A," connect the dots in alphabetical order ending with the letter "Z." Then color the coin.

A Servant's Job

Count the number of feet in the picture. Then answer the question.

How many feet did Jesus wash? _____

I Am the Way

Follow Jesus to find the only path to heaven.

Capturing Jesus

Match the numbers to the pictures to show the correct order of the story.

1

2

3

4

5

Our Sins on the Cross

Cut out the words that describe some of the sins for which Christ died. Then paste them on the cross.

Jesus Is Alive!

Cut and paste the angels inside the tomb. Then finish coloring the picture.

129

My Lord and My God

Connect the dots to see who appeared in the room with the disciples.

130

Share the Good News

Cut out the puzzle from the cutout page. Then put the puzzle together inside the circle.

Cutout Pages

Cutouts for page 9, Lesson 2A

Cutouts for page 43, Lesson 12C

Cutouts for page 52, Lesson 16B

Cutouts for page 105, Lesson 32A

Cutouts for page 121, Lesson 37A

disobedience

selfishness

lying

unkindness

jealousy

Cutouts for page 129, Lesson 40A

Exploring God's Love Scripture Memory

WEEK	SCRIPTURE	DUE DATE	PARENT'S SIGNATURE
1	Genesis 1:1		
2	John 14:15		
3	Proverbs 3:12a		
4	Romans 3:23		
5	Romans 5:8		
6	Proverbs 22:9a		
7	Proverbs 13:15b		
8	Romans 8:28a		
9	Proverbs 28:14b		
10	1 Peter 3:18a		
11	Exodus 20:3		
12	Proverbs 29:25b		
13	Ephesians 2:8		
14	Psalm 143:9		
15	Matthew 5:14a		
16	Psalm 86:7		
17	Proverbs 10:12		
18	Proverbs 1:10		
19	Ecclesiastes 9:10a		
20	Philippians 2:3b		
21	Philippians 2:11		
22	James 4:7		
23	John 3:16		
24	Ephesians 4:32a		
25	Psalm 32:1a		
26	Psalm 56:3		
27	Psalm 119:18		
28	Matthew 22:39b		
29	Matthew 22:37		
30	Psalm 69:33a		
31	John 6:48		
32	John 1:14b		
33	John 10:27		
34	John 6:37b		
35	Romans 10:13		
36	Colossians 3:1a		
37	Ephesians 6:1		
38	Galatians 5:13b		
39	Philippians 2:4		
40	Matthew 28:19a		

PositiveAction
BIBLE CURRICULUM

www.positiveaction.org • (800) 688-3008